Victorian Gardens

Victorian Gardens

Anne Jennings

ENGLISH HERITAGE

IN ASSOCIATION WITH THE MUSEUM OF GARDEN HISTORY

Front cover: **The Terrace, Trentham Gardens, Staffordshire, painted by E Adveno Brooke, 1857**

Back cover: **The joy of wading through a flower meadow makes these Victorian ladies forget their usual decorum. Photograph from the Museum of Garden History's collection**

Published by English Heritage, 23 Savile Row, London W1S 2ET
in association with the Museum of Garden History, Lambeth Palace Road,
London SE1 7LB

First published 2005

ISBN 1 85074 937 X
Product code 50997

A CIP catalogue for this book is available from the British Library

Edited and brought to press by Susan Kelleher
Designed by Pauline Hull
Technical editor Rowan Blaik
Printed by Bath Press

CONTENTS

Introduction

The Victorian period saw Britain's final transition from a rural, agricultural society to one with an urban, manufacturing base, resulting in the country becoming the most powerful industrial nation in the world. Horticulture was directly affected by the resulting innovations and changes throughout the 19th century, from an increased reliance on technology and machinery to a growing fashion for internationally inspired gardens. The eclectic taste demonstrated in Victorian life was evident in gardens of the period, with styles ranging from formal Italianate to a growing interest in 'wild' gardens.

This book explores the multi-faceted character of Victorian gardens, highlighting many of the key horticultural features and fashions of the 19th century. It focuses on some of the most influential individuals of the time, from garden writers to head gardeners, and considers the important role of plants in Victorian gardens. It is clear that our gardening today is still influenced by that of our Victorian forebears, from colourful displays of carpet bedding in urban parks, to interest in international styles.

The book includes a number of practical 'how-to' sections giving detailed advice about creating Victorian-style features in your own garden. Lists of flowering plants, shrubs and trees at the end of the book provide a useful guide for planting in an authentic style. The lists include the availability of the plants, as seeds and container-grown specimens, in UK nurseries.

The flamboyant spires of astilbe, a favourite late Victorian introduction

I

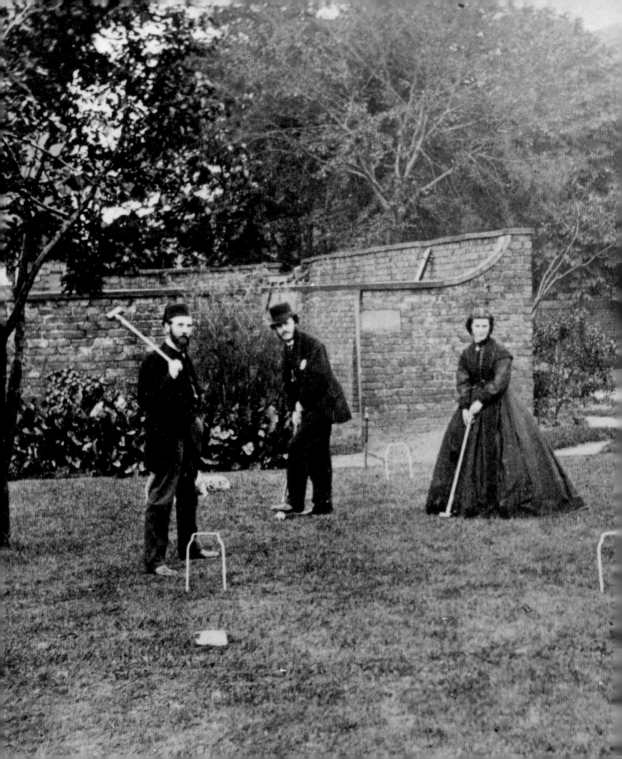

The Victorian period

No other British monarch has ruled as long as Queen Victoria who came to the throne in 1837 at the age of only 19. Her 63-year-reign saw Britain become the world's first industrialised nation, with a vast and ever expanding global Empire that wielded enormous influence. British success underpinned the unprecedented pace and extent of social, scientific and technological change taking place during this period, affecting all aspects of the nation's society and culture. Professional horticulture embraced the innovations with enthusiasm and great creativity, and an eclectic range of Victorian gardens and related activities developed.

One of the greatest social changes of the 19th century was a massive exodus from the countryside, with the nation developing an industrial rather than an agricultural base. As the economy improved, the population rose steadily, providing a cheap and plentiful labour force. The working class gradually abandoned the farms and fields to work in mills and factories, while the middle classes joined professions like banking and insurance. Home ownership became increasingly common among this class who grasped the opportunity to develop fashionable gardens around their new houses and villas.

The gap between rich and poor remained enormous, but by the mid-Victorian period the wealthy often made philanthropic efforts to improve living conditions and provide education

Enjoying a game of croquet, 1866

for the working classes. These included the development of small villages or communities near the factory or mill, built by the owners to house their workers. Sir Titus Salt (1803–76), a philanthropic Yorkshire mill owner built a fine example, called Saltaire in West Yorkshire in the 1850s. Centred round a chapel, and with no public house, these communities reflected the mid-Victorian emphasis on high morals, family values, and Christian teaching. The provision of allotments was just one way that the poor were encouraged to aim for healthy living and self-improvement through hard work, education and abstinence from any form of excess – especially alcohol.

Industrialisation brought enormous benefits to horticulture, ranging from the construction of buildings to the development of specialist tools and equipment. Cheaper, mass-produced materials and new construction techniques were used to build large-span, iron-framed glasshouses heated by sophisticated boilers and hot-water systems. Basic tools such as spades and forks were stronger and more durable than ever before, and glass equipment like cloches were readily available. Glass was becoming more affordable, not only because of cheaper production methods, but also because glass tax was abolished in the mid-19th century. Expansive conservatories, greenhouses and orangeries were built in large gardens, with smaller versions appearing in urban gardens

A selection of conservatories on offer in Boulton & Paul's catalogue, 1895

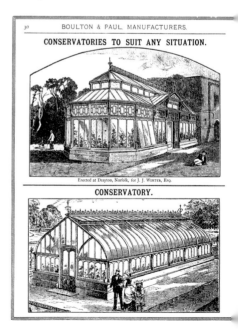

4

or, when space was absolutely at a premium, elaborate glass cases were designed as window boxes.

In 1830 engineer Edwin Beard Budding (1795–1846) adapted a technique used in the woollen industry to produce the first lawnmower. Inspired by the mechanics of a nap-cutting machine, which ran over the surface of woven cloth to provide a smoother finish, he developed the first lawnmower, with blades that cut the grass like a pair of scissors. These early machines were noisy and heavy and needed two men (or a man and a pony) to propel them, but mowing time and labour costs reduced dramatically. Thus began the British gardener's long love affair with the lawnmower:

> To insure the luxury of a 'velvet lawn' is, to speak
> generally, a most easy matter, and although it
> may be comparatively costly in the first instance,
> it will prove in the end one of the best investments
> of gold in gardening.
>
> Shirley Hibberd, *The Floral World*, 1877

Useful and decorative items like path edgings, furniture, and iron, stone and wood features were advertised in gardening magazines and catalogues; publications that were now relatively cheap to produce on the new, steam-powered machines.

Above: **The Victorian glasshouse at Audley End House, Essex**

Below: **A thriving grape vine at Audley End**

plant up a window box

The window boxes used in Victorian homes were placed both indoors and out and varied from a series of individual pots to large containers. Here are a few ideas to reproduce the look of the time.

You need to decide on the sort of compost to use. If you are planting shrubs or long-living plants that will be in the container for more than one season, use a soil-based John Innes No 3 type material. For seasonal plants use a multi-purpose compost supplemented with a slow release feed, and for acid-loving plants like heathers and azaleas use ericaceous compost.

To develop a fully planted look to a window, use a large rectangular terracotta pot across the length of the windowsill. If there is space at the end use two round pots to make sure the whole area is filled.

Line the bottom of the containers with crocks made from broken pots to help drainage and then fill about three-quarters full with compost, packing it down lightly.

Plant a tall specimen in the centre of the container. A young abutilon is suitable, or for drama and late colour, choose amaranthus. For the rest of the planting select lower flowering plants with a 'Victorian' feel, like coleus, begonia, mimulus, calceolaria or mesembryanthemum.

Fill around the plants with more compost and water well. To encourage longer flowering, apply a liquid feed through the season.

Variations:

To create a flowering frame around the window, fix taut wires on the surrounding walls and plant annual climbers at the ends of the container. As the plants grow, tie them into the wires and train them around the window. Effective plants would be *Cobaea scandens*, ipomea, hop and nasturtium.

To increase seasonal interest, change the tall, central plant through summer. Bulbs grown in pots that can be moved in and out of the main container are useful, and the season can begin with *Fritillaria imperialis*, with lilies through summer and then nerine for autumn colour.

wires to support plants

compost

broken pots as crocks

For a shaded window, plant different ferns that will give a very Victorian feel to the planting. Train ivy up and around the wires.

Use a rectangular glass fish tank to create a temporary fern case. As there will be no drainage, it is best to use small ferns, left in their pots with compost filled around, to give the effect that the ferns are planted. Remove the plants and refresh the compost occasionally to ensure the plants do not become waterlogged.

Succulents work well in a very hot situation where small agave, aloe, sempervivum and sedums will thrive.

Look out for antique or reproduction wire plant stands to place in front of the window, inside or out, and use potted plants to extend the theme beyond the window box into the room or onto the terrace.

In addition, daily newspapers like *The Times* and the *Daily Telegraph* became household names after the abolition of tax on newspapers in 1855 and they carried all manner of gardening features and advertisements. Goods ordered through such publications were dispatched by road, rail, canal and, from 1883, via a new postal delivery service.

Although the working classes were enjoying a more comfortable lifestyle by the late Victorian period, it was the middle classes who really had the greatest opportunity for social advancement. Wealthy industrialists who had made their

A pair of pony boots, used to protect the lawn from the pony's hooves during mowing

Keeping the lawns immaculate with a horse-drawn lawnmower at Balmoral, the Scottish home of the royal family bought by Queen Victoria and Prince Albert in 1852

money from mills, factories, mining, and transport were keen to join the ranks of the landed aristocracy and, in an effort to gain acceptance, learnt to wear the correct clothes, appreciate art and music, adopt appropriate manners, and generally acquire an air of gentility. As in previous eras, house decoration and garden layout were two obvious ways to demonstrate taste, power, wealth and education. Indeed the 'new rich' were responsible for creating some of the greatest of all Victorian country gardens. One of the most outstanding was made by Lord Armstrong at Cragside, his Northumbrian home. A lawyer turned industrialist, Armstrong was an inventive genius who was the first person in Britain to have his house powered by hydroelectricity. He also turned his engineering brain to landscape gardening, designing a cast-iron bridge to span the steep valley within the dramatic gardens, and inventing heated pots that revolved to follow the light for the fruit trees growing in the Orchard House in the grounds.

Industrial expansion also brought welcome income to many of the established aristocracy such as the 6th Duke of Devonshire of Chatsworth House in Derbyshire. His inheritance had been dramatically reduced by the extravagances of his predecessor, but income generated by coal mining on his land allowed him to indulge his horticultural extravagances.

A range of lawnmowers to suit the smaller garden

In 1787 William Curtis had first published the *Botanical Magazine* to describe the 'new' plants available to gardeners and this gained increased popularity in the Victorian period. Other horticultural magazines followed, the first notable being John Loudon's *Gardener's Magazine* (1826–44) which was full of information about new gardening techniques, plants and garden design theories:

> *In an art so universally practised as gardening, and one daily undergoing so much improvement, a great many occurrences must take place worthy of being recorded, not only for the entertainment of garden readers, but for the instruction of practitioners in the art.*

J C Loudon, *Gardener's Magazine*, Vol 1, 1826

It was aimed at the professional gardener and, following a merger in 1969, continues to be published today as *Horticulture Week*.

Joseph Paxton's *Horticultural Register* appeared in 1831, followed by his *Magazine of Botany* in 1834. He eventually joined botanist John Lindley (1799–1865) in publishing the *Gardeners' Chronicle* in 1841. This magazine had the aim of being

> *...a weekly record of everything that bears upon Horticulture, or Garden Botany, and to introduce such Natural History as has a relation to Gardening, together with Notices and Criticisms of every work of importance on the subject which may appear.*

John Lindley, *The Gardeners' Chronicle*, 1841

The Horticultural Society began publishing the *Journal* in 1845, (which continues to this day under the title *The Garden*), and *The Cottage Gardener* appeared from 1848 to 1915, appealing to those with an interest in 'outdoor gardening':

> *Utility is our primary object; we wish to improve the gardening of the many and we shall concentrate in our pages the information which will be acceptable and useful to everyone who has space sufficient for a row of cabbages, a row of currant trees, and a flower border ... we shall endeavour to teach them how to grow the most and the best crops on the plot beneath the sway of their spade ...*

The Cottage Gardener, No 1 Vol 1, 1848

As part of his rebellion against elaborate Victorian gardens, William Robinson published *The Garden* (1871–1927), and *Gardening Illustrated* (1879–1956), the latter being aimed at the upper middle class. As well as including articles on practical gardening, plant profiles and garden studies, Robinson took every opportunity to inform the reader about garden design, layout and planting, with the aim of encouraging the creation of 'wild' and 'natural' gardens.

Many other magazines were published during Queen Victoria's reign, including some, like Shirley Hibberd's *Amateur Gardening* (1884), specifically aimed at the amateur market. At the very end of the 19th century, the now well-established and ever-popular *Country Life* was first published.

A page from The Gardening World, 1885, offering a tempting array of advertisements to entice the keen gardener

Gardening as a profession

Wealthy landowners wanted skilled, articulate and educated head gardeners who could cope with the ever increasing demands of running country estates that incorporated fruit, flower and kitchen gardens, exotic planting and conservatories, as well as parkland and woods. To take charge of such diverse areas, head gardeners needed not only horticultural expertise but also the ability to manage large teams of under-gardeners, journeymen, 'improvers', garden boys and labourers.

Gardening became an attractive profession for young boys as it offered training in work with a promising future, as well as providing them with board and lodging throughout their career. The basic 'bothy', where young trainees first lived, gradually improved and by the late 19th century was superceded by more homely lodging houses, often with the aim of keeping the young men away from the alehouse.

Who can wonder that it is difficult – impossible – to keep young men at home in such places [bothies], or that the village or town public-house, or the street with its glare of light and its equally glaring vices, draw men out of such dens to deeper degradation?...By and by higher aspirations will spring forth from the order, quiet, cleanliness, and comfort of the place [the lodging house].

The Garden magazine, 13 January 1872

Terracotta pots were washed by the under gardeners prior to storing

They would have started gardening work as young teenagers, responsible for menial tasks like pot washing, as well as domestic chores such as cooking meals for the other single male gardeners who lived together in the dormitory-style bothy. To reach the position of head gardener would have involved many years learning the craft from the bottom up, working under other gardeners and moving from estate to estate when they were fortunate enough to receive promotion, usually after recommendation from the current head gardener.

Joseph Paxton holding a copy of his Magazine of Botany

Joseph Paxton (1803–65)

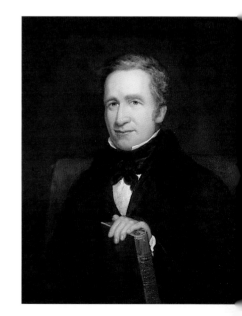

Joseph Paxton holding a copy of his Magazine of Botany

Joseph Paxton was one of the greatest head gardeners of all time and, although his only formal training was as a gardener, he eventually became an architect, engineer, rail entrepreneur and politician. He was appointed as head gardener of Chatsworth House in 1826 and developed a close and mutually respectful relationship with the 6th Duke of Devonshire, who eventually became a keen plantsman. Together they planned and developed the gardens, which had been neglected for many years, creating magnificent new features such as the heated glasshouse known as the Great Stove, and transforming Chatsworth gardens to rank amongst the finest in the country.

Paxton was unusual in achieving the position of head gardener when he was only 23 as it was more common for a head

gardener to be at least 30. By this stage in a horticultural gardening career, remuneration would be relatively high and on a par with the senior household staff. A good standard of housing was also provided for the head gardener and his family, as by now it would be acceptable for him to marry, with his wife often holding a respected position in the house or on the estate.

Paxton's relationship with the Duke demonstrates the important status of the Victorian head gardener who was not considered a menial labourer, but accorded the respect due to any trained professional. Compulsory elementary education for the masses was introduced in the 1870s and public libraries, art galleries and museums were available, free of charge, to encourage poorer members of society to improve their minds. With a more literate working class, the status of traditionally labour-based work gradually improved – with gardening being a fine example.

The Great Exhibition

Right: The vast nave of the Crystal Palace, c 1859

Below: A view of the Crystal Palace at Sydenham, from the south-east

Opposite right: The Mammoth Tree – a 4,000-year-old sequoia from California

Opposite below: A hand-coloured photograph of the Tropical Transept dominated by giant figures of the Egyptian Pharaoh Rameses II

Queen Victoria's German husband, Prince Albert, was a great supporter of British industry. He was the main promoter of the 1851 Great Exhibition at Hyde Park, London – a six-month celebration of British workmanship and manufacturing skills that demonstrated the nation's expertise to a national and worldwide audience. He announced that the aim of the exhibition was '… to show the point of development at which mankind has arrived, and a new starting point from which all nations will be able to direct their future exertions'.

Joseph Paxton, who had been experimenting with large glasshouses and conservatories at Chatsworth, designed the enormous glass and iron structure that housed the Great Exhibition. It became known as the Crystal Palace and was more than six times the size of St Paul's Cathedral, and housed 17,000 exhibitors from

May to October 1851. Over 6,000,000 people visited the Exhibition, many arriving on the new rail network that linked London to the rest of the country, and they made their way through the different courts, transepts and sections of the Crystal Palace each themed with a geographic, historic, or industrial focus.

Profits from the Great Exhibition were used to buy land in South Kensington where the Victoria and Albert Museum and the Natural History and Science Museums were later developed. The Palace itself was bought by Joseph Paxton's company and rebuilt in Sydenham, south London, where a grand new park with elaborate Italianate gardens were laid out around it. The new Crystal Palace became a popular social venue for all classes and hosted many successful flowers shows before it was eventually destroyed by fire in 1936.

Glasshouses and their uses

Under the care of Paxton, and with the enthusiasm and support of the Duke of Devonshire, the Victorian gardens at Chatsworth developed at a dramatic pace. Whenever there was the need to build a glasshouse on the estate, Paxton quickly developed a design and oversaw construction. Working with architect Decimus Burton, he built the Great Conservatory from 1836, and by 1842 the three-quarters of an acre it enclosed was fully planted. This was followed by the construction of the elegant Conservative Wall in 1842, built to house tender climbers and wall shrubs.

Paxton acquired a young plant of the Amazonian water lily, *Victoria amazonica*, from Sir William Hooker of Kew in 1849 and, due to its prolific growth, had to design and build the Lily House specifically to house a pool large enough to grow what would become 140 gargantuan leaves and 112 flowers. The structure of the building was inspired by the ribbed construction of the underside of the lily leaf and this idea was

The glasshouse in the gardens of Osborne House, Queen Victoria's much-loved home on the Isle of Wight

The Conservative Wall at Chatsworth House, Derbyshire, and a plan, drawn in 1850

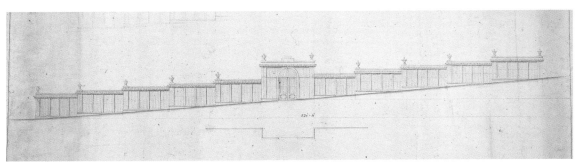

Joseph Paxton's daughter, Annie, stands on one of the leaves of the Amazonian water lily in the Lily House at Chatsworth

influential in his later design for the Crystal Palace. He also created a system that made the water in the pool lap around the lily leaves, mimicking its natural habitat, and such attention to detail was to pay off. Paxton's water lily was the first to flower in Britain, beating its sister plant at Kew and resulting in the presentation of a flower and leaf by Paxton to Queen Victoria herself. The plant was at that time called *Victoria regia*.

Chatsworth's glasshouses were exceptional in their range and scale, but gardening under glass was fashionable, and practised in both large and small gardens by both amateur and professional gardeners. Ornamental displays were created in heated conservatories, where foliage and flowering plants were grown to perfection, in large country houses, public parks, botanic gardens, and in small glass and iron conservatories attached to suburban houses and villas. The plants were grown in densely packed displays, banked high to the back to disguise the shelving systems that supported them. These were year-round displays and, whether created for the private householder or the general public, the pleasant, warm environments were enjoyed from January to December.

The giant water lily known in Victorian times as Victoria regia

Walled kitchen gardens

Large heated greenhouses were a necessity on estates where the 'big house' had to be supplied with food, cut flowers and pot plants. Working glasshouses were often situated within the walled kitchen garden, which was an important working environment where the propagation and cultivation of edible and ornamental plants took place. Walled kitchen gardens had been an essential element in the Georgian country garden but it was the Victorian period, with improving technology and manufacturing processes, that was to see these magnificent places become the hub of the country estate. They were no longer banished to the furthest parts of the garden, but proudly displayed as a demonstration of the head gardener's skill and expertise. He was after all responsible for ensuring an abundant supply of top-quality produce for the family, visitors and numerous staff, all year round.

The gardens became more refined as technology improved and, as understanding of science and horticulture developed, no aspect of the walled kitchen gardens escaped improvement. Enclosed flues were built into walls to heat brickwork and improve production of tender fruits like apricots and peaches. Some walls were designed in a serpentine 'crinkle-crankle' fashion, creating microclimates where the undulated wall reflected heat onto the trained fruit. Specific tools and growing devices were designed for use in the kitchen garden: cucumber straighteners, grape bottles, glass cloches, watering devices and

The recently restored walled kitchen gardens at Audley End House, Essex

A glass cucumber straightener exhibited at the Museum of Garden History, London

forcing pots. Glass was used in innovative ways including removable glass walls that were replaced with shade netting or left open through the summer.

The gardens were laid out in a practical, rather utilitarian way with long, straight paths and geometric beds, but they were also very beautiful environments. Horticultural techniques like training fruit trees as espaliers and cordons, edging beds with clipped box and growing ornamental and edible plants like sweet peas and beans up vertical supports immediately introduced an aesthetic quality to the garden. The architecture of the walls, glasshouses, frame-houses and forcing pits introduced structural elements, while features such as brick or tile path edgings, central dipping pools, and iron fruit tunnels were as attractive as they were practical. Economic necessity saw the end of the walled kitchen garden as a working, productive garden during the early 20th century, but a few survive and several have been restored in recent years. These include the remarkable West Dean Gardens in East Sussex, the organic kitchen garden at Audley End in Essex, and the restored gem at Heligan in Cornwall.

Walled kitchen gardens effectively encompass many Victorian achievements in horticulture and garden design ranging from technological innovation to expertise in the craft of gardening, together with an emphasis on beauty and plantsmanship.

A magnificent espaliered pear tree in a garden in Brighton, Sussex, c 1895

Cottage Gardens

The Victorians had a romanticised view of the past which was demonstrated in all art forms, including gardening. As the rural population migrated to the city, sentimentality about country living increased and the traditional cottage garden, full of 'old-fashioned' flowers such as hollyhocks, pinks and roses, was thought to be idyllic.

> The roadside cottages were gay with hollyhocks and Michaelmas daisies and marigolds, and the bright panes of the windows glittered through a veil of China roses.

Elizabeth Gaskell, *Mary Barton*, 1848

The flowers of the cottage garden were considered a precious relic of the past, threatened with extinction as tastes changed and exotic imports increased in popularity. William Robinson fuelled such fears with his criticism of the high Victorian garden and his loathing of bedding out:

> When, in nearly every private garden in the land, orders to adopt bedding-out in all its severity were given, and the old flowers were consigned to the rubbish-heap without a protest, who saved our precious collections of hardy flowers?

William Robinson, *The Wild Garden*, 1870

'...the little garden...is crowded with a medley of old-fashioned herbs and flowers'

'Minna', *a delightful Victorian painting by Helen Allingham (1848–1926)*

The cottage garden was in many ways a Victorian myth, as the true version would have been far more utilitarian with edible crops for both medicinal and culinary use planted among the flowers. There was in fact a great deal of disagreement about the interpretation of a cottage garden with some insisting that the only true version was the garden belonging to a labourer, while others took it to mean the garden that surrounded a small country house of a higher status, perhaps a farmhouse or villa:

> The porch of this farmhouse is covered by a
> rose-tree: and the little garden surrounding it is
> crowded with a medley of old-fashioned herbs
> and flowers, planted long ago, when the garden
> was the only druggist's shop within reach, and
> allowed to grow in scrambling and wild luxuriance
> — roses, lavender, sage, balm (for tea), rosemary,
> pinks and wallflowers, onions and jasmine, in
> most republican and indiscriminate order.

Elizabeth Gaskell, *Mary Barton*, 1848

The horticultural propaganda that surrounded the part-myth of the Victorian cottage was powerful enough to stand the test of time, and the style is still regarded with affection today, with many people considering it typical of the English country garden.

An informal mix of flowering plants gives a feel of the Victorian cottage garden

Ornamental gardens

Whether using 'old' or 'new' money, early Victorian landowners continued the 18th-century tradition of creating parkland and expansive lawns around their homes. However, the Georgian idea of the 'natural' landscape, did not appeal as much as the concept of artistry and, perhaps more importantly, plantsmanship. Different landscape styles developed as technological innovations, modern techniques, and an increasing number of new plants were introduced throughout the period. Just as Stephen Switzer and Charles Bridgeman had eased the transition from formal 17th-century styles to the more open landscapes of the early 18th century, and Humphry Repton had re-introduced the concept of the flower garden in the late Georgian period, so J C Loudon was to be the link figure who assisted the transition from the landscape park back to ornamental gardens and gardening.

John Loudon (1783–1843)

John Claudius Loudon was a Scot who studied landscape design in Edinburgh, beginning his career in London when he was only 20 years of age. He quickly developed an impressive client list and travelled throughout the country undertaking commissions. Wherever he went, he was inspired by a new idea or project and as a result soon published a number of influential gardening books on a wide range of horticultural subjects. His didactic style was well received and Loudon eventually became

Ornamental gardens at Castle Combe, Wiltshire

Engraving of J C Loudon, 1845

one of the foremost commentators and advisors of the time on both private and public gardens, large and small.

Loudon's key principle for garden and landscape design was that artistry should be supported by an equal emphasis on good horticultural practice. This extended from maintaining an immaculate garden to asserting dominance over nature by using techniques such as grafting. John's wife, Jane, wrote posthumously about how her husband had been intrigued by the practice of grafting an ornamental woody plant like a rose onto an orange tree. He had seen this in Italy in 1819 when he visited the traditional Italian Renaissance gardens that so appealed to his love of formal landscape design.

Loudon could perhaps be described as an 'honest' garden and landscape designer. He detested any attempt at deception or pretence that gardens were anything but contrived artistry. A good example is his criticism of the popular but romanticised view of the cottage garden (see p 27), and his loathing of the early Victorian fashion for rustic adornment, ranging from flower baskets to summerhouses. These were built of rough timber or tree stumps and were often planted with ferns and ivy or thatched with moss. Loudon considered that such features 'deceive[d] the spectator, and make him believe that the scene produced is of a fortuitous origin; or produced by the humble exertion of nature'.

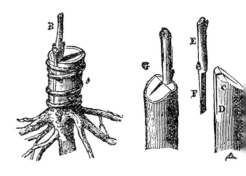

Grafting techniques shown in Gardening Illustrated, *6 September 1879*

A rustic seat advertised in a garden magazine

Complex debates that had centred round the late 18th-century Picturesque landscape spilled over into the early decades of the 19th, and Loudon was influential in adapting the style to suit early Victorian horticulture and tastes. He favoured Repton's formal terraces and architectural design near the house but, moving out toward the wider landscape, introduced almost exclusively non-native and exotic plants, or specimens that had obviously been trained or adapted.

The thatched hermitage at Frogmore, Berkshire, designed in the popular rustic style

Loudon wanted to emphasise that man, not nature, had created the garden landscape and recommended that trees and large shrubs should be planted in island beds, either in isolation or with significant areas of bare soil between them. This ensured that each specimen could be appreciated for its individual beauty, and great care was taken in positioning each one to ensure a sense of unity, balance and even symmetry and geometry. Such ideas formed the basis of the style he referred to as 'Gardenesque', a term that became widely used thanks to regular features in Loudon's *Gardener's Magazine* – although it was eventually applied to a variety of 'artificial' garden styles and often related solely to the use of non-native plants. He wrote that

> … in all works of art, and in all natural objects which are to be examined singly, one of the greatest beauties is symmetry…those trees and shrubs which he manages in a gardenesque manner brought into the most perfectly symmetrical forms, by tying the branches up or down, inwards or outwards as may be necessary, with small, almost invisible, copper wire …

> J C Loudon, *The Suburban Gardener and Villa Companion*, 1838

Formal Victorian-style bedding at Brodsworth Hall, South Yorkshire

create a summer bedding display

Although time-consuming and potentially expensive, it is fun to plant a small section of a garden with a seasonal carpet of colour. Choose self-contained areas such as the borders running along a front path, or a small bed next to a patio. A sunny site is best although some bedding plants like Busy Lizzies grow well in more shaded areas.

The ground should be well dug first and all the perennial and annual weeds removed, and then lots of organic matter needs digging in. The area should be trodden and raked several times after digging to ensure a level surface and a fine tilth, then a light sprinkling of fertiliser applied.

You can either draw a design on paper as a scale plan which will help you calculate the number of plants needed, or you can simply mark out the design on the soil. Trickle sand along lines drawn in the soil with a cane so you can assess the pattern and make any changes before planting. Until you become experienced, stick to simple patterns and geometric lines.

The choice of plants is up to you and your personal preference for bright, hot colours or soft pastel shades. Think about the final height of plants and make sure tall specimens are planted at the back. It is a good idea to include some foliage plants to provide a change of texture and colour.

Bedding schemes will need to be watered on a daily basis in hot weather and given a liquid feed every two weeks throughout the season to ensure continual flowering. Keep the bed free of annual weeds and clip over any vigorous foliage plants regularly. Here are some 'recipes' which work well.

Striking colours:

Scarlet pelargoniums, lime-green nicotiana, purple (non-trailing) lobelia and the acid yellow leaves of helichrysum, clipped regularly through the season to keep the plants compact.

Hot colours:

Orange and yellow marigolds, orange and yellow plumes of celosia, red verbena (non-trailing) and bright green foliage of *Bassia scoparia f. trichophylla* syn. *Kochia trichophylla* (Burning bush) for contrast.

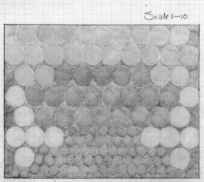

Pastel shades:

Lilac petunia, pink brachyscome, pale blue ageratum, silver leaved senecio.

Parterre:

Plant a permanent box hedge as a border or simple parterre and infill with seasonal colour.

Plant spring bulbs and forget-me-nots in autumn for spring colour.

Texture:

Use tight, hummock-forming plants, for example sempervivum, saxifrage, sedum, acaena, and raoulia for a textured design.

Raoulia haastii   Sedum spathulifolium
Raoulia hookeri   Saxifraga moschata 'Cloth of Gold'

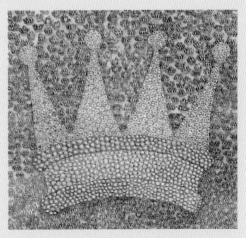

Public parks

Basic principles of the Gardenesque style were frequently applied to the increasing number of public parks. Loudon was directly involved with many of these, for example, designing the recently restored Derby Arboretum in 1838. From the start of his career, Loudon petitioned for the creation of public green spaces in cities and as early as 1803 wrote an article entitled *Hints on Laying Out the Ground in Public Squares*:

> *Our continental neighbours have hitherto*
> *excelled us in this department of gardening;*
> *almost every town of consequence having its*
> *promenades for the citizens en cheval and also*
> *au pied. Till lately, Hyde Park, at London, and a*
> *spot called The Meadows, near Edinburgh were*
> *the only equestrian gardens in Britain; and*
> *neither were well arranged.*

J C Loudon, *Encyclopaedia of Gardening*, 1822

Paternalistic attitudes towards the poor, together with general concern about cramped and unhygienic conditions in towns, played a part in the development of the Victorian public parks that remain such important green spaces today. The parks were free and available to all classes, providing space for healthy recreation and a distraction from the evils of the

The Aviary, Derby Arboretum

public house and music hall. Industrial benefactors often funded the creation of parks to encourage workers to take part in healthy pastimes and provide the opportunity for them to observe the manners and behaviour of educated, wealthy members of society.

The Public Park movement began slowly around the 1830s when Battersea Park and Hackney's Victoria Park in London joined the long established Royal Parks, although the latter were only occasionally open to the public. During the later 19th century, greater momentum was seen in the north where industrialisation was more intense, and by the 1840s, Preston, Derby and Birkenhead parks had opened. Acts of Parliament in the 1850s accelerated the pace of development and industrial cities like Birmingham, Manchester, Leeds and Liverpool soon followed.

Great names in Victorian horticulture, including John Loudon, Joseph Paxton and his one-time apprentices, John Gibson and Edward Kemp, were at the forefront of park design which reflected many late 18th-century ideas. Long circuitous paths, some for use by pedestrians and others for carriages, ran around and through the whole park landscape with large groups of trees hiding features or routes that could then be discovered. Trees were planted to educate as well as please and lakes were another essential element, as seen in Loudon's

A hand-coloured photograph of the intricate bedding schemes at Victoria Park, London

Derby Arbortetum. Here, undulating mounds of earth gave the illusion of an expansive landscape while large rockeries, open lawns and islands in the middle of artificial lakes all reflected elements of the Picturesque and later Gardenesque landscape.

Parks gradually became more formal in layout during the 19th century and modern planting styles, like carpet bedding and sub-tropical and exotic schemes that demonstrated Britain's power of exploration, were displayed at ambitious and competitive levels. The lower middle classes visited parks to gain inspiration for their own gardens where planting styles were copied on a smaller scale.

Bedding schemes were often designed as a tribute to Queen Victoria, and other commemorative features included fountains and statues. Bandstands, park lodges, elaborate iron railings and gates, boathouses, tea-rooms and the like were all designed and built with great care and attention to detail, and added to the recreational facilities incorporated into the landscape. Conservatories, palm houses and display greenhouses, using modern heating systems and construction materials like glass and iron, allowed the Park Superintendent and his team to show off their horticultural skills as well as providing places for public recreation in inclement weather.

A busy day in Hyde Park, London. Rotten Row is packed with horse-drawn vehicles and Lady's Mile is in the background, 1870–1900

oudon's interest in public landscapes extended beyond parks and in 1829 he drew up a plan to ensure that London, and other developing towns and cities, would incorporate green space into fast-increasing developments. Although his London plan was never implemented, many of his ideas are reflected in modern planning regulations – for example his recommendation for a protected green zone around towns is similar to the 'green belts' that surround cities today.

Wherever a country town is likely to extend beyond a diameter of half a mile, we think a zone of breathing ground should be marked out as not to be built on, for the sake of the health of the poorer part of the inhabitants ....

J C Loudon, *Hints on Breathing Places for the Metropolis, and for Country Towns and Villages, on Fixed Principles*, 1829

Many of Loudon's publications were aimed at the ever-expanding middle class and he had a particular interest in the gardens surrounding villas in newly developing suburban areas. The factory or mill owner, together with professionals such as doctors and lawyers, needed easy access to town or city workplaces but did not want their families to live in polluted urban environments. The development of luxurious houses surrounded by large gardens on the outskirts of towns introduced the concept of suburban living. One of Loudon's

'...the cheerful aspect of vegetation; the singing birds in their season; and the enlivening effect of finding ourselves unpent-up by buildings...'

Rosa 'Louise Odier', introduced during the Victorian period

popular books, *The Suburban Gardener and Villa Companion* (1838), aimed to educate garden owners about the design, planting and care of their sites and gave detailed instructions on the layout of gardens categorised by size under his headings of first, second, third and fourth-rate gardens to indicate the social and financial status of the owner.

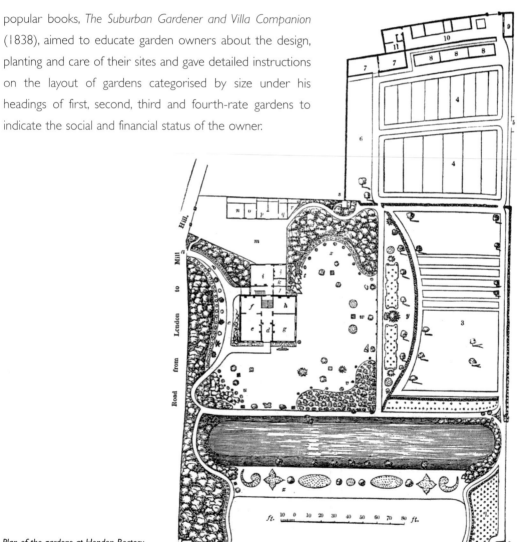

Plan of the gardens at Hendon Rectory in the suburbs of London

*The enjoyment to be derived from a suburban
residence depends principally on a knowledge of
the resources which a garden, however small, is
capable of affording. The benefits experienced
by breathing air unconfined by close streets of
houses, and uncontaminated by the smoke of
chimneys; the cheerful aspect of vegetation; the
singing birds in their season; and the enlivening
effect of finding ourselves unpent-up by buildings,
and in comparatively unlimited space; are felt by
most people....*

J C Loudon, *The Suburban Gardener and Villa Companion*,
1838 (third-rate gardens)

Hendon Rectory

Jane Loudon (1807–58)

John's wife, Jane, is an important Victorian gardening figure in her own right. She provided support for her husband who was not in good health and her assistance in his work became essential after his right arm had to be amputated following a series of illnesses. She accompanied him on his many journeys throughout Britain, wrote up his notes and, after starting out as a fantasy novelist, became a garden writer. Her market was middle-class women and she encouraged her audience to pick up tools and take part in practical gardening. Jane's first gardening book and encyclopedia, *The Ladies' Companion to the Flower Garden* (1840), was closely followed by *Gardening for Ladies*, which was full of practical advice and instruction for gentlewomen gardeners. She also published a short-lived monthly magazine *The Ladies' Flower-Garden* (1843–4), produced as themed volumes that included Hardy Biennials, Herbaceous Perennials and Hothouse Plants. Here is her advice on soil preparation:

Jane Loudon, who not only supported her husband in his work, but was an influential garden writer in her own right

> It must be confessed that digging appears at first sight a very laborious employment, and one particularly unfitted to small and delicately formed hands and feet; but, by a little attention to the principles of mechanics and the laws of motion, the labour may be simplified and rendered comparatively easy….

Jane Loudon, *Gardening For Ladies*, 1840

The working class increasingly found opportunities to garde

Historical styles

John Loudon's emphasis that man, not nature, created garden landscapes, opened the door to a revival of interest in Italianate and Tudor gardens. This led to the restoration of historic gardens such as the one at Levens Hall in Cumbria where the long neglected Tudor topiary was regenerated to spectacular effect. It was however in the recreation and adaptation of historical styles that Victorian gardeners excelled and, even though the layout and design of their gardens was often retrospective, the planting style and choice of specimens was to be unmistakably Victorian.

The work and skills of the architect and the garden designer were to become inextricably linked from the mid-Victorian era onwards and by the Edwardian period the two would be, in garden history terms, almost inseparable.

Sir Charles Barry (1795–1860)

One of the most notable Victorian architects working in this shared arena was Sir Charles Barry, whose dramatic work at Trentham Park in Staffordshire has been restored. Here, Barry designed wide terraces with Italianate statuary, stone urns and an elaborate fountain, together with a 17th-century style parterre filled with 19th-century style carpet bedding.

Barry also designed a parterre garden in a dramatic coastal setting at Dunrobin Castle in Sutherland, Scotland, as well as

The Italian gardens at Trentham Park, Staffordshire

49

at other great country houses including Cliveden in Buckinghamshire, Shrubland Park in Suffolk and Harewood House in Yorkshire.

Topiary in the gardens of Levels Hall, Cumbria

William Andrews Nesfield (1793–1881)

An associate of Barry's, William Nesfield became a dominant influence in the fashion for French-style parterres with his elaborate designs being eagerly sought by the rich. His commissions extended beyond parterres to other landscape and garden designs and included work at Castle Howard in Yorkshire, the Royal Botanic Gardens at Kew and Holkham Hall and Blickling Hall in Norfolk. Although he was famous for colourful schemes that combined bedding plants with box hedges, such as in the Avenue Gardens in Regent's Park, one of his most beautiful designs is at Broughton Hall in Yorkshire. It relies on the colour, texture and pattern of the hedge alone for impact and its scrolling, serpentine pattern lies in a sunken garden where it can be viewed from a raised walkway.

The elaborate parterre designed by Nesfield at Broughton Hall, Yorkshire

Bedding and exotic planting schemes

Increasing availability of tender bedding plants provided designers like Nesfield with the material to create fashionable carpets of colour. Not only had the plant hunters been busy introducing new species to Britain, but hybridisers were 'improving' flowering plants and developing strains suitable for bedding out. Technological advances ensured that these new plants could be grown by the thousands, supplying designers with sufficient to furnish their schemes.

Mass-produced iron- and timber-framed glasshouses of every shape and size could be reliably heated by coal-fired boilers that supplied hot water to a network of cast-iron pipes. New methods of glass manufacturing produced large sheets of bubble-free glass at about the same time that the tax on glass was abolished. In combination with these developments, the supremacy and skill of the head gardener meant that the era of carpet bedding schemes had truly dawned. Complex and elaborate patterns were designed and planted, and what began as a two dimensional art form developed into three dimensional by the 1890s, with features like crowns, vases and rolls of carpet created from wire frameworks packed with soil and studded with a dense covering of plants.

Professional gardeners in public parks, fashionable seaside resorts and botanical gardens all experimented with designs and plant combinations. The fully working floral clock at the entrance

Exotic planting style is still popular today

53

to Princess Street Gardens in Edinburgh is still decorated with seasonal plants today and many seaside towns continue the tradition of using carpet bedding displays on promenade walks.

One attraction of this [carpet bedding] system, and one which, apart from the universal love of rich colours, has done much towards making it popular, is the ease with which the most pleasing designs can be worked out with the aid of alternantheras, coleuses, centaureas, pyrethrums, cerastiums, succulents, and other dwarf foliage plants, while as to the diversity of the designs themselves, there is no practical limit.

Thompson's Gardener's Assistant, 1884

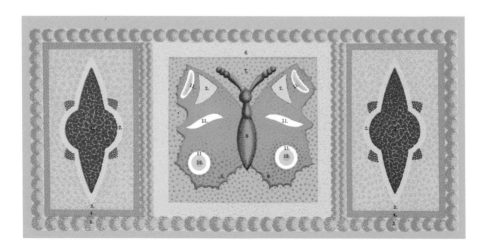

Carpet bedding schemes, although in many ways typical of high Victorian gardening, were not universally popular. One alternative that still provided seasonal colour and interest without the reliance on low, stiff carpet bedding, was sub-tropical planting, fashionable in the mid to late 19th century. Island beds and borders were 'bedded out' with a wide range of exotic plants, including bananas, caladiums, canna, and coleus, which proved to be highly demanding in terms of preparation and cultivation. Plants had to be cared for under glass during the cold months of the year, the ground dug and prepared and, once bedded out, they needed regular watering, feeding, staking and tying. One of the most famous places to see sub-tropical planting was in Battersea Park in South London where the Park Superintendent, John Gibson, was the acknowledged expert.

Carpet bedding at Cragside, Northumberland

The introduction of large-foliaged or stately-habited plants into our open-air flower-gardens during the summer months enables us to obtain pleasing and varied glimpses of luxuriant tropical vegetation, otherwise unattainable in our northern climate.... In order to obtain the best effects in colour an abundance of fresh green foliage is required and this greenery is agreeably augmented by stately tropical plants....

Thompson's Gardener's Assistant, 1884

William Robinson (1838–1935)

A plantsman famous for his 'naturalistic' garden style, Robinson was initially inspired by a development of the sub-tropical planting style during a visit to France. He noticed how vulnerable exotic plants were replaced with more weather-resistant, hardy specimens that still echoed the character and style of the tender specimens. Robinson's work started a horticultural rebellion against formal Victorian garden styles, and although he used the term 'wild garden' to describe his planting style, he incorporated a high proportion of non-native plants into woodland and flower gardens. Robinson's loose, informal planting schemes were to be highly influential in the early decades of the 20th century.

create an exotic planting scheme

The effect of an exotic planting scheme can be effectively created by using both familiar and more unusual non-native plants. They work best in an island bed or a long border and the ground needs to be thoroughly prepared first. However, remember that some of the plants will have been grown in large pots so you might need to be a little more vigorous in your initial digging to ensure sufficient soil depth. Be very generous with the organic matter and fertiliser as these will be very demanding plants!

Choose tall, substantial plants for the back of borders or in the centre of island beds. These will also provide a structural element to the planting scheme and should be repeated in groups along a border. For flowering plants try canna, rheum or datura, and for foliage use banana, castor oil plant, rhus or Chusan palm. Plant around the structural plants with more delicate-looking specimens like abutilon or melianthus and also use tall annuals

like *Nicotiana sylvestris* and masses of *Verbena bonariensis*.

Now think about adding some colour using selected forms of dahlia, which will need staking, and the leaves of phormium or cordyline. Bamboos will also add to the effect of the scheme. As you move forward, bring in shorter specimens like agaves, caladium and elegant grasses like pennisetum. Amaranthus, or love-lies-bleeding, will add a touch of drama.

Keep experimenting with these planting schemes and think about including other annuals like eschscholzia and sunflowers to complement the theme and don't forget about bulbs like eucomis, large alliums, lilies and gladioli.

Water and feed throughout the season. Dead-head where necessary and be prepared to tie plants into stakes as they grow.

International influence

New plants continued to arrive in Britain in massive numbers from every continent of the world and the different ways they were used demonstrates the eclectic character of Victorian horticulture. Some were potted-up and packed onto conservatory benches or used as individual specimens in the house, but many new arrivals were destined for outdoor rather than indoor cultivation. Unlike the exotic and tender plants that were used in seasonal schemes, hardier specimens were incorporated into mixed borders and shrubberies, some being planted in geographically zoned areas in both botanic and large private gardens with the aim of recreating the character of the environments from which they originated.

Cornish gardens were as important in Victorian Britain as they are today for, thanks to the county's mild climate, tender plants such as aeonium and tree ferns thrive outdoors, often without protection. Much of the soil in this extreme western county is ericaceous so acid-loving plants like rhododendrons and azaleas grow well. These conditions have long provided perfect environments in which to create magnificent and distinctive gardens where mass plantings of dicksonia, gunnera, camellias and other dramatic plants thrive. Gardens like Glendurgan, Trebah, and Mount Edgecumbe and, perhaps most dramatic of all, Tresco Abbey Gardens across the waters on the Scilly Isles, were made in the Victorian period and can

Gunnera manicata, a popular plant from South America

A rhododendron in full bloom

still be visited today. Gardens with similar planting styles were created in other areas of Britain where mild micro-climates exist, most notably at Bodnant in North Wales and Logan Botanic Garden, Stranraer, warmed by the Gulf Stream.

It is however the gardens of Biddulph Grange in Staffordshire, created in 1850s, that best demonstrate the importance of non-native plants and international architecture on Britain's gardens during the Victorian period. Wealthy and knowledgeable, Biddulph's owner James Bateman (1811–97) and his wife Maria built and planted a series of gardens within a garden, each with a geographical theme. Hard landscaping, architectural features and planting combined in varying proportions to create the character or impression of different countries or geographical locations around the world. The Egyptian garden, for instance, relies on yew topiary and stone, whereas the Chinese garden displays an interpretation of the Great Wall of China, a temple, pagoda and bridge, surrounded by plants from the region. Parts of the garden such as the Pinetum, Arboretum, Dahlia Walk and Rose Garden concentrate purely on plants while others, like the Glen and Stumpery made of uprooted tree stumps, introduce natural architectural materials. The house and terrace are predominantly Italianate, and the whole garden is held together by yew hedges, mass planting and structural features providing a gentle transition from one area to the next. The

An arch in the Quarry Garden at Belsay Hall, Northumberland

gardens are now under National Trust ownership and have been fully restored.

Rock gardens at Biddulph, and other important gardens around the country such as Belsay Hall in Northumberland, aimed to recreate the character of mountainous regions of the world and reflected the Victorian fascination with nature. They were enormous structures that demanded large-scale planting, and groups of coniferous trees, mountain ash, banks of rhododendrons and other large shrubs were used. Discussions about the Picturesque landscape included debates about rock gardens – should the rocks be laid in a natural or contrived fashion?

One of the most dramatic rock gardens, still in existence today, was made at Chatsworth House between 1842 and 1848, under the supervision of Joseph Paxton. The route through the rock garden takes the visitor past an initially modest collection of rocks, then on by the 'Matterhorn' to a seemingly precarious collection of mammoth stones balanced one on top of the other that form a roof across the path that invites (often nervous!) visitors through. Other features such as waterfalls, a placid pond and moving rocks on hidden turntables were incorporated into the area, with the crowning glory being the gigantic Wellington rock.

Plants

For the first time in garden history, the role of the scientist vied with that of the plant hunter in introducing new plants to British gardens. When scientists like Charles Darwin began to publish their theories and findings, the horticultural world was as eager as any to absorb and apply new information in a practical way. Darwin rocked the Christian establishment with new and dangerous theories in which he claimed that nature rather than God was responsible for human evolution. His theories also applied to plants and included scandalous ideas about their sexual reproductive systems, describing how male pollen fertilised the female ovule to produce viable seed and that plant variations

> ... may be attributed to the male and female reproductive elements having been affected prior to the act of conception...the chief [reason] is the remarkable effect which confinement or cultivation has on the functions of the reproductive system...how many cultivated plants display the utmost vigour, and yet rarely or never seed! In some few such cases it has been found out that very trifling changes, such as a little more or less water at some particular period of growth, will determine whether or not the plant sets a seed.

Charles Darwin, *On The Origin of Species*, 1859

Forms of canna lily were introduced in the Victorian period and used in fashionable exotic planting schemes

Fascination with science and the increasing understanding and appliance of its theories had an enormous impact on 19th-century gardening. Darwin and other British and international scientists observed the natural world in minute detail, appreciating for the first time the similarities between the reproduction of plants and animals. Understanding such fundamental information led to attempts to produce bigger, brighter, longer-lasting plants and flowers and plants by crossing them. Eventually this science developed into one that provided amateur and professional growers with healthy, disease resistant and, especially important in the case of edible crops, enormously productive plants. The heated debates that surrounded early Victorian revelations about plant reproductive systems and people's manipulation of them can in many ways be likened to today's arguments about issues such as GM crops.

As the Victorian period progressed, gardeners and nurserymen were keen to apply this new scientific understanding to their work, and information dispersed through gardening books and magazines was eagerly received. Experimentation was carried out in all aspects of horticulture from pruning and training woody plants to pest control and appreciation of soil science. Nevertheless, it was plant breeding that held most fascination and, although some work had been carried out in the 18th century, it was the Victorian era that applied scientific understanding rather than more random experimentation.

Charles Darwin in about 1857

A Victorian lady almost swamped by an extravagant display of chrysanthemums, 1897

Botanic gardens and nurseries

Another demonstration of the partnership between gardens and science can be seen in the growing number of botanic gardens that were being created throughout the Victorian period in large cities such as Birmingham (1832), Sheffield (1834), Cambridge (1846) and Bristol (1882). Although some of these were linked to university education and research, many were accessible to the public and supported the Victorian ideals of self-education and healthy recreational activity. Ness Botanic Garden in Liverpool was founded and funded in 1898 by Arthur Kilpin Bulley, a cotton-mill owner who used his substantial wealth to create a garden that was partly open to the public. The Royal Botanic Society's popular garden, designed by Robert Marnock was created in Regent's Park's Inner Circle in 1872, and continued until the lease expired in 1932.

'...it is universally admitted that, for arrangement, and for securing the enjoyment of both visitors and exhibitors, no place as yet equals "The Park"'

Few public gardens were ever made on less favourable ground than that of the eighteen acres, the site of the Botanic Garden in Regent's Park; and no public garden of the same size has, notwithstanding obvious defects, been more admired for the excellence of its design....As many as 17000 persons have endeavoured to find room on its pleasant little lawn; and even now, not withstanding the many counter attractions at Kensington, the Crystal Palace,

Forms of water lily were arriving in England throughout the 19th century

67

and elsewhere, it is universally admitted that, for arrangement, and for securing the enjoyment of both visitors and exhibitors, no place as yet equals 'The Park'.

The Garden magazine, 3 February 1872

The Palm House at Kew, designed by Decimus Burton

In 1841 the Royal Botanic Gardens in Kew changed from sovereign to government ownership and Sir William Hooker (1785–1865), founder of the *Botanical Magazine* (1826) and Professor of Botany at Glasgow University, was appointed Director, remaining in his post until his death. Hooker had been a great admirer of his predecessor Sir Joseph Banks (1743–1820), but in the 20 years since Banks' death, the garden had suffered severe decline. Hooker was determined to restore the gardens to their former glory and make Kew the foremost botanical garden in the world. His great contributions to the garden's development, included commissioning architect Decimus Burton to design a heated glass building that would house exotic plants, and the Palm House remains one of the greatest surviving Victorian glass and iron buildings anywhere in the world. Hooker also allowed public access to the garden for the first time and ensured gardeners were properly trained and educated, providing a reading room and library for their use. Some of the Kew-trained gardeners would later be commissioned by the Director to collect new plants from overseas for the garden and glasshouses at Kew.

Hooker was succeeded as Director by his son, Sir Joseph Dalton Hooker (1817–1911), who was a botanist and plant collector with a specific interest in rhododendrons (he collected R. thomsonii from the Himalayas). On his retirement in 1885, Joseph's son-in-law and his Assistant Director, Sir William Thiselton-Dyer took over the post until 1905 and, although he was responsible for the creation of the rock gardens and alpine house, Thiselton-Dyer is perhaps most famous for allowing the first women gardeners to train at Kew.

Joseph Dalton Hooker, Director of Kew and a close friend of Charles Darwin

With so many eager recipients awaiting their new introductions, plant hunters travelled to all corners of the world seeking out new garden and botanical specimens, including 'commercial' plants such as rubber and cocoa. Plant hunting gradually became a professional pursuit no longer undertaken exclusively by keen amateurs but increasingly by paid plant hunters whose trips were funded by botanic gardens, private garden owners or commercial nurseries. Of the latter, the most famous was Loddiges of Hackney whose cultivation and propagation of non-native plants had played an essential part in the development of British horticulture over the last 200 years. Owner George Loddige supported

Three of Kew's early female gardeners, dressed as men to prevent 'sweet-hearting' with their male colleagues

Nathaniel Ward in the development of the Wardian Case that proved to be a major turning point in the successful transportation of non-native plants to Britain, as the sealed case provided ideal conditions in which living plant material could be shipped from its natural habitat to the glasshouses of Britain.

Unlike Loddiges, the Veitch nursery, which was originally established in Devon but eventually expanded to London, survived through the Victorian period and became one of the most active plant introducers of the 19th century. It eventually commissioned over 20 collectors, including the brothers, William and Thomas Lobb, and in the very late Victorian period, Ernest 'Chinese' Wilson.

The public appetite for new plants was insatiable and no sooner had a plant been introduced than pressure was on to make it available to gardeners the length and breadth of the nation. Professional gardeners would exchange plants and share recently acquired specimens with other growers, but once commercial nurseries obtained a plant it would be propagated as quickly as possible to ensure it could be supplied to the general public. Such nurseries placed advertisements in magazines like the *Gardeners' Chronicle*, describing new plants and promoting availability.

The Wardian Case displayed at the Museum of Garden History, London

A selection of new plants that were brought to England in the Victorian period: a. Athurium magnificum; b. Cycas revoluta; Pandanus Veitchii; d. Phormium tenax variegatum; e. Lilium auratum; f. Saracenia Flavia picta; g. variegated lily of the valley

An advertisement in the Gardeners' Chronicle, 10 May 1851

CANTUA DEPENDENS *OR* BUXIFOLIA

A BEAUTIFUL NEW HARDY GREENHOUSE PLANT FROM PERU

MESSRS. VEITCH AND SON have the greatest satisfaction in offering to the Public, the above lovely plant from the Andes of Peru, where the flowers are so much esteemed by the natives that they adorn their chambers with them on feast days. It was again exhibited at Chiswick on 3rd of this month and was then awarded the highest prize given for new plants

❧ THE SILVER GILT MEDAL ☙

It is a plant of neat habit and foliage, blooms freely in a small state and may be kept in a cold pit or frame through winter, being of about the same hardiness as Fuchsia, and as easy of cultivation: from its novelty and beauty it will be an acquisition to every collection and be cultivated by every florist. It is figured in Curtis's 'Botanical Magazine' for this month and will also shortly appear in Paxton's 'Flower Garden'. Good established plants will be sent out on and after 12th June at 21s each, with the usual discount to the Trade.

Horticultural societies and shows

The Horticultural Society, founded in 1804, became a significant force in both amateur and professional gardening and, from the 1820s, also commissioned plant hunters to bring specimens back to its Chiswick garden before financial problems took their toll. Prince Albert, the Society's President, in an effort to support the Society through its financial difficulties and provide it with a more accessible garden for the public to enjoy, helped to arrange a move from its Chiswick site. He granted a lease on 20 acres of land in Kensington where William Andrews Nesfield designed an extravagant Italianate-style garden with a beautiful glass conservatory, or winter garden, at the northern end. The gardens were officially opened in 1861, the same year that, prior to his death in November, Prince Albert granted royal consent to change the Society's name to the Royal Horticultural Society. When the lease expired less than 30 years later, the RHS returned to Chiswick until air pollution forced the final move to Wisley in 1903. The South Kensington gardens were eventually replaced with buildings that include the current Imperial College, now part of the University of London.

The Horticultural Society instigated the earliest flower shows where prize blooms, fruit and vegetables were exhibited. The first was held in Chiswick in 1827, although later competition from Paxton's Crystal Palace Flower Show, and the more accessible event organised by the Royal Botanic Society in

The gardens of the Royal Horticultural Society at Kensington

Regent's Park, proved more popular with the public and so added to the Society's financial difficulties.

In many ways the formation and development of the Royal Horticultural Society ensured that gardening became a highly organised and well-promoted activity at both amateur and professional level. The layout and design of gardens and landscapes had long been an obsession with British gardeners – but usually one that only the wealthy could enjoy. Through the Victorian period, however, lower middle class and eventually working class people began to garden for pleasure. The latter in particular found growing plants an affordable and fascinating pastime with a previously unimaginable range available to them. Then, as now, gardening was a way of escaping from the pressures and difficulties of day-to-day life and became a crucial part of many people's lives, rich and poor alike.

Opposite: **Dahlias remain as popular today as they were in the Victorian period, with none as widely grown as Dahlia 'Bishop of Llandaff'**

A John Hill of Wiltshire, surrounded by Toogood Seeds awa:

Plant lists

The following list of plants, while not exhaustive, give an indication of plants that were popular in Victorian Britain. Only those of interest to the gardener have been included so crops and 'non-ornamental' plants are excluded. All the plants listed are available either as seed, container-grown plants or as bare-rooted trees and shrubs. You might find that some of the plants are not readily available in their Victorian forms. It is crucial then to decide whether your planting must be authentic or whether it is to be 'in the style of' Victorian planting, in which case you will have a wider palette to select from and will find the plants easier to obtain.

Many cultivated forms of plants are only available as container-grown specimens because they are often propagated vegetatively, for example as cuttings or by layering. However, most annuals and many British wild flowers, native or naturalized, are rarely sold in garden centres as established plants because they are short-lived and uneconomical to grow on a commercial scale. You will have to grow such plants from seed obtained from specialist suppliers.

Please remember that under the Wildlife and Countryside Act it is illegal to uproot any wild plant and to take material from protected species. All the plants listed in this book are available from legitimate sources.

A Victorian illustration showing a range of flowering conservatory plants

BOTANICAL NAME	COMMON NAME	PLANTS	SEED
Summer bedding			
Aeonium arboreum ssp. atropurpureum	Dark purple houseleek tree	Unusual	Available
Antirrhinum majus	Common snapdragon	Many cultivars available	Widely available
Echeveria secunda		Unusual	Available
Echeveria secunda var. glauca	Glaucous echeveria	Unusual	Available
Erysimum cheiri	Common wallflower	Many cultivars available	Widely available
Gazania rigens	Treasure flower	Unusual	Available
Helichrysum petiolare	Liquorice plant	Unusual	Available
Impatiens walleriana	Busy Lizzie	Many cultivars available	Many cultivars available
Lobelia erinus	Edging lobelia	Many cultivars available	Available

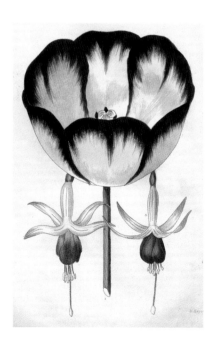

Far left: **Gazenia splendens**

Left: Green's Victoria Regina tulip and Harrison's Madonna and Goldfinch fuchsias from Floricultural Cabinet, October 1843

BOTANICAL NAME	COMMON NAME	PLANTS	SEED
Mesembryanthemum crystallinum	Common Ice plant	🪴	🌱
Pelargonium – many including 'General Tom Thumb', 'Lord Bute'		🪴	🌱
Sempervivum tectorum	Common houseleek	🪴	🌱
Senecio cineraria	Silver ragwort	🪴	🌱
Tagetes erecta	African marigold	🪴 Many cultivars available	🌱 🌱
Tagetes patula	French marigold	🪴 Many cultivars available	🌱 🌱
Tradescantia zebrina	Silver inch plant	🪴	🌱
Verbena x hybrida		🪴 Many cultivars available	🌱 Many cultivars available

Exotic and sub tropical planting

Abutilon pictum 'Thompsonii'		🪴	🌱
Agave americana	American aloe	🪴 🪴	🌱
Begonia coccinea	Angelwing begonia	🪴	🌱
Canna indica	Arrowroot	🪴	🌱 🌱
Canna iridiflora		🪴	🌱
Dahlia coccinea	Scarlet dahlia	🪴	🌱
Fatsia japonica	Japanese aralia	🪴 🪴	🌱
Melianthus major	Honey flower	🪴 🪴	🌱
Musa basjoo	Japanese banana	🪴 🪴	🌱
Nicotiana tabacum	Common tobacco plant	🪴	🌱
Paulownia tomentosa (coppiced)	Foxglove tree	🪴 🪴	🌱
Phormium tenax	New Zealand flax	🪴 🪴	🌱
Ricinus communis	Castor oil plant	🪴	🌱
Tropaeolum speciosum	Flame flower	🪴 🪴	🌱

BOTANICAL NAME	COMMON NAME	PLANTS	SEED
Conservatory and greenhouse plants			
Bougainvillea spectabilis		Cultivars available only	
Calceolaria integrifolia	Slipperwort	🪴	Many cultivars available
Campsis grandiflora	Chinese trumpet creeper	🪴	📦
Celosia argentea var. *cristata*	Chinese wool flower	🪴	📦
Citrus aurantium	Seville orange	Cultivars available only	📦
Cobaea scandens	Cup and saucer vine	🪴	📦 📦
Fuchsia magellanica var. *gracilis*	Hardy fuchsia	🪴	📦
Fuchsia 'Timlin Brened'		🪴	📦
Heliotropium arborescens	Common heliotrope	🪴	📦
Lapageria rosea	Chilean bellflower	🪴	📦

Far left: **Fuchsia gracilis**

Left: **Sempervivum tectorum**

BOTANICAL NAME	COMMON NAME	PLANTS	SEED
Musa acuminata	Commercial banana	Many cultivars available	
Nerium oleander	Oleander	Many cultivars available	
Pelargonium – doubles, 'fancies', gold and bronze leaved, zonal and ivy leaved including 'Crystal Palace Gem', 'Dolly Varden', 'A Happy Thought'.			
Pelargonium 'Prince of Orange'	Pelargonium 'Prince of Orange'		
Pelargonium crispum	Lemon geranium		
Pelargonium odoratissimum	Apple geranium		
Plumbago auriculata	Cape leadwort		
Trachelospermum jasminoides	Confederate jasmine		

Garden plants
Bulbs & herbaceous

Anemone hupehensis var. *japonica*	Chinese anemone		
Aster novae-angliae	New England aster		
Camassia quamash	Common camassia		
Cortaderia selloana	Pampas grass		
Delphinium elatum	Candle larkspur		
Gunnera manicata	Chilean rhubarb		
Helenium autumnale	Autumn helen flower		
Lupinus polyphyllus			
Nepeta racemosa	Raceme catnip		
Nerine bowdenii	Bowden-Cornish lily		
Papaver orientale	Oriental poppy		
Phlox drummondii	Annual phlox		
Thalictrum aquilegifolium	French meadow rue		

BOTANICAL NAME	COMMON NAME	PLANTS	SEED

Shrubs & climbers

BOTANICAL NAME	COMMON NAME	PLANTS	SEED
Berberis darwinii	Darwin's barberry		
Buddleja globosa	Orange ball tree		
Ceanothus americanus	Indian tea		
Ceanothus thyrsiflorus	Blue blossom		
Clematis montana	Mountain clematis		
Clerodendrum bungei	Glory flower		
Clianthus puniceus	Lobster claw / Parrot's bill		
Cornus kousa	Kousa		
Escallonia rubra var. *macrantha*	Chilean gum box		
Fuchsia magellanica	Lady's eardrops		
Garrya elliptica	Silk tassel bush		
Griselinia littoralis	Broadleaf		
Hamamelis mollis	Chinese witch hazel		
Hebe cupressoides			
Hebe hulkeana	New Zealand lilac		
Hydrangea macrophylla 'Mariesii'			
Hypericum calycinum	Rose of Sharon		
Ligustrum japonicum	Japanese privet		
Olearia avicenniifolia			
Olearia traversii	Ake-ake		
Pieris formosa		Many cultivars available	
Ribes speciosum	Fuchsia-flowered currant		
Rosa moyesii			
Vitis coignetiae	Crimson glory vine		

BOTANICAL NAME	COMMON NAME	PLANTS	SEED
Trees			
Acer palmatum 'Dissectum Atropurpureum'		🪴	✉
Acer rubrum	Red maple	🪴 🪴	✉
Aesculus x carnea		🪴	✉
Betula pubescens	Downy birch	🪴	✉
Betula pendula 'Youngii'	Young's weeping birch	🪴 🪴	✉
Catalpa bignonioides	Indian bean tree	🪴 🪴	✉
Chamaecyparis lawsoniana	Lawson's cypress	🪴 Many cultivars available	✉
Fagus sylvatica 'Pendula'	Weeping beech	🪴	✉
Magnolia macrophylla	Large-leaved cucumber tree	🪴	✉

The National Pelargonium Collection (all groups including species)

Fibrex Nurseries Ltd, Honeybourne Lane, Pebworth, Stratford-upon-Avon, Warwickshire, CV37 8XP

Scoring system

Unusual = Not listed for sale in the *RHS Plant Finder* or *The Seed Search*

Available = available from up to 29 listed nurseries

Widely available = Available from over 30 listed nurseries

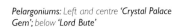

Pelargoniums: Left and centre **'Crystal Palace Gem'**; *below* **'Lord Bute'**

Further reading

Campbell, Susan *Walled Kitchen Gardens*. Princes Risborough: Shire, 1998

Campbell-Culver, Maggie *The Origin of Plants*. London: Headline, 2001

Clifton, R T F (editor), *Decadic Pelargonium Cultivars: Based on the Spalding List of Pelargonium Cultivars Names: 1840–1959*

Conway, Hazel *Public Parks*. Princes Risborough: Shire, 1996

Davies, Jennifer *The Victorian Flower Garden*. London: BBC Books, 1991

Davies, Jennifer *The Victorian Kitchen Garden*. London: BBC Books, 1987

Desmond, Ray *Kew, the History of the Royal Botanic Gardens*. London: Harvill Press, 1995

Devonshire, Duchess of *The Garden at Chatsworth*. Ted Smart, 1999

Elliott, Brent *The Royal Horticultural Society*. Chichester: Phillimore, 2004

Elliott, Brent *Victorian Gardens*. London: Batsford, 1986

Fearnley-Whittingstall, Jane *The Garden, An English Love Affair*. London: Weidenfeld and Nicholson, 2002

Hobhouse, Hermione *The Crystal Palace and the Great Exhibition*. London: Athlone Press, 2002

Hobhouse, Penelope *Plants in Garden History*. London: Pavilion, 1992

Quest-Ritson, Charles *The English Garden. A Social History*. London: Penguin Viking, 2001

The RHS Plant Finder

Published annually by the Royal Horticultural Society, the *Plant Finder* lists more than 65,000 plants available from 800 nurseries as well as contact details, maps and opening hours for all the nurseries listed. There is also an online version of the *Plant Finder* on the RHS website: www.rhs.org.uk

The Seed Search

Now in its 5th edition, *The Seed Search* lists over 40,000 seeds available from 500 seed suppliers, with details of where to find them. It also includes 9,000 vegetable cultivars. Compiled and edited by Karen Platt, and online: www.seedsearch.demon.co.uk

Useful organisations and societies

The Museum of Garden History
The Museum of Garden History exists to enhance understanding and appreciation of the history and development of gardens and gardening in the UK, and was the world's first museum dedicated to this subject. Its attractions include a recreated 17th-century knot garden with historically authentic planting and collections of tools and gardening ephemera, as well as a well-stocked library.

www.museumgardenhistory.org

The Garden History Society
The Garden History Society aims to promote the study of gardening, landscape gardens and horticulture, and to promote the protection and conservation of historic parks, gardens and designed landscapes and advise on their restoration. The Society runs a series of lectures, tours and events throughout the year.

www.gardenhistorysociety.org

The Royal Horticultural Society
The RHS is the world's leading horticultural organisation and the UK's leading gardening charity dedicated to advancing horticulture and promoting good gardening. It offers free horticultural advice and a seed service for its members and has plant centres at its four flagship gardens.

www.rhs.org.uk

The National Council for the Conservation of Plants and Gardens
The NCCPG seeks to conserve, document, promote and make available Britain and Ireland's garden plants for the benefit of horticulture, education and science. Its National Plant Collection scheme has 630 National Collections held in trust by private owners, specialist growers, arboreta, colleges, universities and botanic gardens.

www.nccpg.com

The Hardy Plant Society
With over 40 local groups in the UK, the Hardy Plant Society encourages interest in growing hardy perennial plants and provides members with information on both familiar and rarer perennial plants, how to grow them and where to find them. Its annual seed list is available for members to use and contribute to.

www.hardy-plant.org.uk

The Henry Doubleday Research Association
HDRA is a registered charity, and Europe's largest organic membership organisation. It is dedicated to researching and promoting organic gardening, farming and food. The HDRA's Heritage Seed Library saves hundreds of old and unusual vegetable varieties for posterity, also distributing them to its members. The HDRA currently manages the kitchen garden at Audley End, Essex, for English Heritage and runs Yalding Organic Gardens (see Places to visit).

www.hdra.org.uk

Centre for Organic Seed Information
Funded by DEFRA and run by the National Institute of Agricultural Botany and the Soil Association, the Centre for Organic Seed Information is a 'one-stop shop' for sourcing certified-organic seed from listed suppliers. It covers fruits, vegetables, grasses, herbs and ornamental plants among others.

www.cosi.org.uk

Local gardens trust and national plant societies
Almost all counties and regions of the UK have their own gardens trusts and most genera of plants have a national society. Your local groups may have fundraising plant sales or a members' seed list that you could join.

Places to visit

Alton Towers
Alton
Staffordshire ST10 4DB
Tel: 01538 702200
www.towerstimes.co.uk/rides/gardens/
gardens

Audley End House
Audley End
Saffron Waldon
Essex CB11 4JF
Tel: 01799 522399
www.english-heritage.org.uk

Battersea Park
Albert Bridge Road
London SW11
www.batterseapark.org

Belsay Hall, Castle and Gardens,
Belsay,
Newcastle upon Tyne,
Northumberland NE20 0DX
Tel: 01661 881636
www.english-heritage.org.uk/belsay

Biddulph Grange Garden
Grange Road
Biddulph
Staffordshire ST8 7SD
Tel: 01782 517999
E-mail:biddulphgrange@nationaltrust.org.uk
www.nationaltrust.org.uk

Birkenhead Park
The Grand Entrance,
Park Road North,
Birkenhead
Merseyside CH41 4HD
Tel: 0151 652 5197
www.visitliverpool.com

Blickling Hall
Blickling
Norwich
Norfolk NR11 6NF
Tel: 01263 738030
E-mail:blickling@ntrust.org.uk
www.nationaltrust.org.uk/places/blickling

Bodnant Garden
Tal-y-Cafn
Colwyn Bay
Conwy
Wales LL28 5RE
Tel: 01492 650460
E-mail:office@bodnantgarden.co.uk
www.bodnantgarden.co.uk

Brantwood Garden
Coniston
Cumbria LA9 5JD
Tel: 015394 41396
E-mail:enquiries@brantwood.org.uk
www.brantwood.org.uk

Brodsworth Hall and Gardens,
Brodsworth,
Doncaster,
South Yorkshire DN5 7XJ
Tel: 01302 724969
www.english-heritage.org.uk/brodsworthhall

Castle Howard
York
North Yorkshire YO6 7DA
Tel: 01653 648444
E-mail:curator@castlehoward.co.uk
www.castlehoward.co.uk

Chatsworth House
Bakewell
Derbyshire DE45 1PP
Tel: 01246 565300
www.chatsworth-house.co.uk

Cliveden House
Cliveden
Taplow
Maidenhead
Berkshire SL6 0JA
Tel: 01628 605 069
E-mail:Cliveden@nationaltrust.org.uk
www.nationaltrust.org.uk

Cragside House
Rothbury
Morpeth
Northumberland NE64 7PX
Tel: 01669 620150
E-mail:cragside@nationaltrust.org.uk
www.nationaltrust.org.uk

Crystal Palace Park
Thicket Road
Penge,
London SE20 8DT
Tel: 020 8778 9496
www.bbc.co.uk/london/yourlondon/
crystal-palace

Derby Arboretum
Arboretum Square
Osmaston Road
Elvaston
Derby
Derbyshire
Tel: 01332 716272.
www.derbyarboretum.co.uk

Dunrobin Castle
Golspin
Sutherland
Scotland KW10 6RR
Tel: 01408-633177
E-mail:dunrobin.est@btinternet.com
www.gardens-scotland.co.uk

Glendurgan Garden
Mawnan Smith
nr Falmouth
Cornwall TR11 5JZ
Tel: 01326 250906
E-mail:glendurgan@ntionaltrust.org.uk
www.nationaltrust.org.uk

Harewood House
Harewood
Leeds
West Yorkshire LS17 9LQ
Tel: 0113 218 1010
E-mail:info@harewood.org
www.harewood.org

Holkham Hall
Wells-next-the-Sea
Norfolk NR23 1AB
Tel: 01328 710227
E-mail:enquiries@holkham.co.uk
www.holkham.co.uk

Places to visit

Logan Botanic Garden
Port Logan
Stranraer
Wigtownshire
Scotland DG9 9ND
Tel 01776 860 231
E-mail:logan@rbge.org.uk
www.rbge.org.uk/rbge/web/visiting/lbg

**Mount Edgecumbe House &
Country Park**
Cremyl
Torpoint
Cornwall PL10 1HZ
Tel 01752 822236
E-mail:mt.edgecumbe@plymouth.gov.uk
www.mountedgecumbe.gov.uk

Osborne House
Osborne,
Isle of Wight PO32 6JY
Tel: 01983 200022
www.english-
heritage.org.uk/osbornehouse

Oxburgh Hall
Oxburgh
King's Lynn
Norfolk PE33 9PS
Tel: 01366 328258
E-mail:oxburgh@nationaltrust.org.uk
www.nationaltrust.org.uk

Regent's Park
London NW1 4NR
Tel: 020 7486 7905
E-mail:hq@royalparks.gsi.gov.uk
www.royalparks.gov.uk/parks/
regents_park/

Shrubland Park
Coddenham
Ipswich,
Suffolk IP6 9QQ
Tel: 01473 830 221
E-mail:enquiries@shrublandpark.co.uk
www.shrublandpark.co.uk

Tatton Park
Knutsford
Cheshire WA16 6QN
Tel 01625 534400
E-mail:tatton@cheshire.gov.uk
www.tattonpark.org.uk

Trebah Garden
Mawnan Smith
Cornwall TR11 5JZ
Tel 01326 250448
E-mail:mail@trebah-garden.co.uk
www.trebah-garden.co.uk

Trentham Gardens
Trentham
Stoke-on-Trent
Staffordshire ST4 8AX
Tel: 01782 657341
E-mail:enquiry@trenthamleisure.co.uk
www.trenthamleisure.co.uk

Tresco Abbey Gardens
Isles of Scilly
Cornwall TR24 0QQ
Tel 01720 422849
www.tresco.co.uk

Waddesdon Manor
Waddesdon
nr Aylesbury
Buckinghamshire HP18 0JH
Tel: 01296 653211
www.waddesdon.org.uk

West Dean Gardens
West Dean
Chichester
West Sussex PO18 0QZ
Tel: 01243 818210
E-mail:gardens@westdean.org.uk
www.westdean.org.uk

The walled garden, Osborne House

Acknowledgements and picture credits

English Heritage and the Museum of Garden History would like to thank the many individuals who contributed to this volume, in particular Rowan Blaik for technical editing, James O Davies for photography, as well as colleagues at the National Monuments Record for picture research. Thanks to the Royal Botanic Gardens, Kew, for allowing access to the gardens for photography and to Livvy Gullen for further research.

The author would like to acknowledge the invaluable assistance of Jane Wilson, Fiona Hope and Philip Norman at the Museum of Garden History.

Unless otherwise stated, images are © English Heritage or © Crown copyright. NMR. All English Heritage photographs taken by James O Davies except for 5, 60, 89. Original artwork by Judith Dobie.

Other illustrations reproduced by kind permission of: Bridgeman Art Library: 26 (Chris Beetles Ltd., London, UK), 67 (John Bethell); Broughton Hall: 50; David Austin Roses: 42; Devonshire Collection, Chatsworth, reproduced by permission of the Chatsworth Settlement Trustees: 14, 15, 19, 20, 21; Director and the Board of Trustees of the Royal Botanic Gardens, Kew: 71; John Critchley 35; Museum of Garden History: 2, 4, 8, 9, 11, 23, 24, 25, 30, 32, 33, 40, 44, 46, 47, 48, 54, 65, 72, 73, 76, 78, 80, 82, back cover; National Pelargonium Collection: 85; National Portrait Gallery, London: 31; National Trust: 55; Royal Horticultural Society, Lindley Library: front cover, 45, 74; Stephen Robson 52.

Every effort has been made to trace copyright holders and we apologise in advance for any unintentional omissions or errors, which we would be pleased to correct in any subsequent edition of the book.

About the author

Anne Jennings is a freelance garden designer, consultant and writer, and Head of Horticulture at the Museum of Garden History. She is the co-author of *Knot Gardens and Parterres*, published by Barn Elms, and writes for a variety of gardening magazines.

Other titles in this series

Roman Gardens
Medieval Gardens
Tudor and Stuart Gardens
Georgian Gardens
Edwardian Gardens